MORE WORDS –
Pointers to the Truth of Oneness

Graham Stew

Published in 2016 by FeedARead.com Publishing

Copyright © The author as named on the book cover.

The author or authors assert their moral right under the Copyright, Designs and Patents Act, 1988, to be identified as the author or authors of this work.

All Rights reserved. No part of this publication may be reproduced, copied, stored in a retrieval system, or transmitted, in any form or by any means, without the prior written consent of the copyright holder, nor be otherwise circulated in any form of binding or cover other than that in which it is published and without a similar condition being imposed on the subsequent purchaser.

A CIP catalogue record for this title is available from the British Library.

For Lana

PROLOGUE

I owe an introduction to you, dear reader, in order to orientate you to the book which you have opened. This book can stand alone as a collection of ramblings and reflections (I can hardly call them poems) with the broad theme of non-duality. It follows on from my first book, 'Too Simple for Words' (O-Books, 2016) which addressed aspects of non-dual teaching, and in language which tried to avoid the jargon and obscure terminology which is commonly found in spiritual texts.

By way of summarising the core elements of this wisdom (found in the heart of all religions and spiritual traditions) the following may help:

1. There is only Oneness – all distinction and concepts are made by the mind.
2. Within this one living Awareness, consciousness arises to create all apparent 'things'.
3. All phenomena, including the concepts of time and space, are limited mental constructions and ultimately unreal.
4. What is Real never changes, has no qualities, and thus cannot be described.
5. We are that Awareness, but have become lost in our stories of being separate individuals.
6. Understanding who we really are, and living in the light of that Knowing, is the purpose of human life.

Even stating these six points is seen as hopelessly inadequate, and a reminder that words alone can never capture this Understanding. So why write another book? To be honest, I have no idea ... but the words keep coming.

Let me emphasise this: these words are nothing but pointers ... rough indicators of the direction that the mind can take to examine and rid itself of delusion and ignorance. Finally, the mind has to give up, let go of all concepts, and rest in the simplicity of Being.

So who needs books like this one?

When I see the billions of humans on this planet lost in the illusion of separateness, protecting and defending fictitious identities, and the conflict and suffering that results - there is my answer.

I do not apologise for the differing repetitions of this message throughout the pages that follow ... the meaning can be expressed in various ways, but the insight is always the same. The poking of ignorance in different places may make it finally shift out of the way!

So I hope the words that follow may help you in your journey towards realising who you really are, and the discovery that you are already home.

Bon voyage!

More words ... who needs them? These words are simply Life whispering to Itself. If Life doesn't wish to end its game of 'hide and seek', It will pretend not to understand or even express any interest.

If Love does want to end the game, there will be a shout of "Found you! ... you were here all the time!". No more words will be needed.

The magic show may continue, but without the belief that anything personal is involved. We will have simply left our seats in the cinema, and joined the Projectionist!

Truth needs no definition ...
No dry dictionary description.
Truth is the humming aliveness inside the skin ...
The incessant flow of thoughts and sensations –
Always now.

Seeing the light shining on the pen;
Hearing its rustle as it moves across the paper.
Touching the page to keep it open –
such a gentle pressure.
Just these things ... and the Awareness that
holds them all with a calm curiosity.
This is where Truth can be found.

THINKING

The factory of thought….
The source of dreams …
Re-cycler of words …
Fossilising ideas into dead knowledge.
Killing learning with theory.

Who is the culprit?
Our mind – you say?
… and do we *have* a mind?
If it's mine, why can't I control it?
Think only nice thoughts;
enjoy pleasant emotions?
Switch it off when sleep is needed?

What is this mind? … a rattle-bag of words;
Relics of the past …
A collection of memories cobbled together
To create the story of 'me'.
A prison without locks …
a cell with an open door.
Step outside –
with the emptiness that contains all.

Look back – where is the mind now?
Vanished – it never was more than
an old, dead word …
an invention of psychology.
Without mind to gather them up
and claim ownership
thoughts arise and float on by …
coming from and returning to
the Silence that watches …
the Awareness that holds and loves everything.

WORDS

Words are pictures from the past,
Tools to build ideas upon;
Building blocks of theories.

Words inhabit thoughts –
Populating our minds with images,
Memories and dreams.

Words form languages;
Creating meaning…
Fostering communication.

Words can caress or kill;
Heal or hurt;
Develop or divide.

They label and clarify,
Producing objects out of sensations;
Freezing the flow of living into
Dead blocks of letters and sounds.

Captives in their own mental prison,
Words conspire to escape
the confines of their own activity.

Ideologies, opinions, beliefs –
all are made of words;
in-breeding more compulsory dogma.

Abandoning concepts – words fail;
cease their chatter,
and fall silent.

Words can only point in the right direction;
The rest of the journey must be made
without a map.

The Silence from which words arise
breathes in division... breathes out peace;
and ... wordlessly ... whispers of Love.

DREAMING

Enjoying a good dream;
Enduring a bad dream ...
So our life goes.
But when do we wake up?
How do we know what is Real?
The fire in the house is extinguished
by opening the eyes ...
Look around ... the room is still here;
A sigh of relief ... what a nightmare!

The day begins ... another dream –
of separation, ambition, emotion...
memories, plans, fantasies...
Is this Real, or am I dreaming?
When will I truly wake up?

Safe inside its chrysalis ...
the caterpillar
dreams of flying

Silence is defined by its absence;
the movement of the body ….
the chatter of the mind.
We fill silence with manic activity;
keeping emptiness at bay
with compulsive doing.

The void terrifies us;
the dread of nothingness
drives us to fill our days with dross.
A futile struggle against death …
but the wise embrace it all:
The drive to become;
The illusion of control;
The unfolding story of Life.

Consciousness finding Itself …
energy moving through form.
The wild miracle of being
emerging from,
and returning to Silence.

No need for words …
Butterfly loving a flower
In silence.

Energy: flowing - playing;
Taking the form of thoughts, motions, sensations.
Moving the wind,
Beating the heart,
Holding the world within vibrating awareness.

Uncreated, undying;
Assuming form after form;
Cheating death and performing tricks
in the playground of Life.

This is all we are;
Have been - ever will be;
Meaningless … hopeless,
but an expression of perfection … just this!

Clouds

The sky-like mind contains clouds;
passing weather –
white, grey and black
… all shades are welcome.

Sometimes pretty and enchanting;
sometimes gloomy and threatening.
All clouds tell a story

as they pass by.

Clouds obstruct the view ...
demand attention
with imagined substance;
claiming a reality that deceives.

Clouds live in our minds
as thoughts and perceptions;
Appearing as real ...
but disguising Reality.

Leave them alone ...
enjoy the view;
love their variety;
but don't be fooled into believing they're real.

We contain the clouds...
they appear in us;
and when they leave we are untouched.
We remain blue, infinite ... joyous.

Windy day ...
Seagulls chasing clouds;
What fun!

Light uncovers darkness.
Wisdom reveals ignorance
... and so the weather of our
lives twists and turns its way
between our days of progress,
and our nights of regress...
Of finding and losing the path
through the woods...
Stumbling past the trees
that can teach and also obstruct.
They teach by endurance and patience
but obstruct the light
that could illuminate our way.

The imaginary path that leads
to where we started from
... our beginning we discover
to be our ending.
The light we seek is inside,
quietly shining in stillness;
The visions we follow are mind made;
Conceptual follies.
Rest ... here in presence –
and allow the brilliance
of Truth to shine forth
and give you Peace.
Light ... without darkness,
outside duality...
only Peace shines.

We call it a garden ... but it is no 'thing';
This buzzing spectacle of colours,
shapes and scents
is just energy playing with itself.
No subject or object ... no separation –
We are what appears in awareness.
We are the blossoms entertaining bees;
We are the butterflies exploring the plants,
and the eggs they lay are ours.
The bees' fumbling delight
Is our own drunken dance.
New shoots, withered leaves;
Birth and death ... all is here
In this amazing display;
Appearing Now ... as Love greeting Life.

Sunflowers
in the plum tree -
laughing at the poor fruit!

Our lives are as dewdrops
forming in the mysterious
night of our souls ...
Glittering in the brilliant
Light of our dawn;
Shrinking in the heat of experience...

Until our essence evaporates;
To return whence it came...
a wave falling into the sea –
a dewdrop slipping into
the River of Life.

We change – as figures of salt
swimming in the sea ...
intent on our separate journeys;
but softly dissolving ... disappearing;
not ceasing, but ceaselessly changing.

Sunny morning ...
insects drinking from a dewdrop
before it vanishes.

The mountain of Truth has many paths
leading to its summit.
Some straight upwards ...
arduous and challenging.
Others gently hair-pinning up
and around the slopes.
The destination is the same for all the routes.

Many don't even start the climb;
Preferring the security of the dark valleys.

Those who do attempt the ascent
Find captivating sights along the way
and stay there ... imagining
They have found the finest view.

Some climbers tackle unstable rock-faces,
and fall back afraid,
never to climb again.
Others ascend too quickly ...
find the rarefied atmosphere,
clear light and space too unsettling...
and settle for a cave on the mountainside.

So many different paths ...
All claiming to be the best;
Promising the easiest climb.

Climbers on each path may meet,
Exchange experiences; compare notes;
and change their course.
Others will argue and even fight
over whose path is the truest.

Of course, the view from the summit
is the same for every climber;
... and those who really SEE
will know that they have not moved and inch;
and realise that their journey was a dream
from which they have finally awakened.

Rain drops on rock ...
How slowly the
Mountain dissolves!

As painters use canvas
so musicians paint on silence.
The space between the notes
is what God sounds like.

Silence is the glass which holds
the wine of music ...
The medicine of the mind
which is above and beyond all words.

Music vibrates in the memory;
Shaking off the dust of everyday life ...
Being to the soul
what water is to the body.

Our cares are blown gently away by the
breeze of music ...
The poetry of the air.
So much like a prayer;
Without music Life would surely be a
mistake.

When the mind falls silent
and concepts drop away;
What remains, holding all
in a warm embrace ...
is Love

When muscles fail and eyesight dims
what supports us to the
end of our story, and beyond ...
is Love.

When petals fall
and leaves wither
what drives new Life
and Springtime growth ...
is Love.

The driving clouds,
the heaving sea;
all the dancing joy of the universe ...
is moved by Love.

Butterfly...
Frantic to lay her eggs
Does she know it's autumn?

LOVE

Poor, abused word ....
demeaned, degraded, belittled;
Excuse for selfish dependence ....
Crutch for grasping egos ...
'Love' should not be used lightly.

Love should be whispered;
Glimpsed in the cloisters of cathedrals;
In the notes of a symphony ...
In the flowering of a rose.

In the meeting of two souls;
When consciousness knows itself;
Abandoning boundaries ... dissolving self;
There ... if you don't label it ...
There you can find Love.

But then, never to use the word?
As Love does not exist separately.
Love contains all that exists...
Is all that exists;
And now let us be quiet.

When the One becomes many
There is lost an innocence,
Falling through the air like a heavy feather.

When the many appear as clouds of foes,
We lose ourselves in otherness.

Life's music drifts closer,
Once the mind doesn't engage in judgement.

The light from the window embraces all,
Once the curtains disappear.

Rainbows come from white light,
Split by the prism of rain.
So consciousness is split
into countless specks;
Appearing as you and me ....
as a toad and as a tree.

Life coming and going as
a multitude of forms ...
United in our essence; but fooled into
a sense of helpless separation.

Look beyond the appearances
that dazzle and create distinctions.
See the unity that ties all things ...
The beating energy of Life
That enjoys acting all the parts
In this marvellous drama!

JUST KISS THE MIND GOOD NIGHT

Children playing with soap bubbles ...
How they drift and soar –
Empty planets on the run,
Rising to meet the sun;
To kiss the breeze, avoiding trees.
Reflecting spheres of rainbows,
Following where the wind goes;
Until ... like our lives,
So quickly gone ...
Before begun ...
These floating holes
Pop into nothingness.

Joy and sadness need each other –
our sorrows carve the hole in our souls
that Joy can fill.

Joy as deep as the ocean ...
our troubles as light as its foam.

All the tears of our story disappear
amongst the waves; and
their salt melts into oblivion.

Our task is to live with amazement;
breathless in awe of the simple
miracle of being here.

Moving beyond human loves and hates
to touch the heart of Joy;
to smile at the source of happiness ..
to move with the natural flow of the
universe...

and to make our lives into
poems of new joys.

Today the wind is shaking the trees ...
Sending birds tumbling across the sky
in an ecstasy of disarray.

It has been windy before;
Autumnal chill has visited the houses
and gardens for many years past.

Yet this is new ...
Colours, sounds, feelings....
Never been before;
the slap of fresh innocence
across the face of familiarity.

Energy is moving ....
Patterns in form....
and form from emptiness;
Life is unfolding anew.

The wind insists on attention,
reminding us of its impermanence;
Its invisible power ...
We wait for it to sleep.

A pointless vigil,
for wind never rests ...
Moving from tender, caressing breeze,
to frightening, bruising storm.

So Life moves, too ... in this eternal Now;
Appearing as all things ... from nothing ...
Until the desire for oblivion
Allows us to let go.

To let go of plans, memories;
all that is conceptual –
and fall into the silent un-knowing
where Love is waiting.

---

*We are nothing ....
and now,
Take nothing away!*

In the half-light of dusk
the sun and the moon
compete over lighting the world.

God and Goddess in mortal combat, or
heavenly dance...
knowing that one will have to
hide behind the earth until the morning.

And so the daily pas-de-deux continues –
apparently without end...
but the universe is changing.

Planets are born; others burn out;
our sun will cool and fade...
and the curtains will close
on the light of the world.

Such cosmic dramas appear in awareness,
a watching that is self-illuminating,
self-revealing - destroying
the darkness of ignorance
with the Light of Love.

---

*Who is there
to win or lose?
.... this human race!*

Eternity – the concept
that defies imagination.
How can time halt its breathless rush into
the future?
And rest in the still point of calm?
Outside time and space there is stillness
for restless waves of emotion and thought -
peace for the chattering mind.

Sweet oblivion for the weary travellers;

What can eternity offer but
This ... Now ... outside time?
The kiss of sunshine on autumn flowers ...
The smiles of garden birdsong ...
A surprising heaven.

It's called *'samsara'* ...
this staggering side-show
that performs for our perception.
Amazing mirage of radiant insubstantiality.
It captivates with drama,
entertains with theatre.

The manifestation of the moment,
rising and falling without
leaving a trace.
As nothing lasts, there is
nothing to lose or hang onto ...
simply the play of phenomena,
appearing in the light of awareness.

In silent simplicity, the dance
and the dancer disappear
into the dancing.
It is miracle enough to walk upon this earth
... and take this next breath.

So what is this 'ego' of ours?
This ghostly critic – the illusory nag
that showers us with 'shoulds' and
'shouldn'ts'

Just a mask of separation
... a trick of self-consciousness,
leading to a game of 'make-believe';
and the loss of our early innocence.

Unless born with fresh vision ...
Aware of awareness; lost in fascination with
the chaotic confusion of Life
and one with our surroundings.

Eating from the Tree of Knowledge,
we are educated into dualism ...
a 'hand-me down' view of a piecemeal reality;
and the delusion of self is born.

The ego is our prison cell
which we decorate with the cosmetics
of possessions, status and achievement.
Trapped inside a conceptual identity,
we never see that our cell door is wide open.

Freedom from ego's tyranny
Is simply a step away;
the universe is only expanded Self –
let go of ego... and the universe becomes 'I'.

The mind arises from the ego,
the ego from consciousness;
trace the source of the ego
and find Love!

Moonlight at midnight –
ghostly glistening on a silver sea;
borrowed sunlight, surprisingly bright.
Flower, shrub and tree
appear in shades of grey.
Guardian of our sleep,
the moon creeps silently across the sky,
escaping from the approach of morning.
But captured in a puddle of rainwater –
the face on the moon smiles up at us –
dissolving all separation.

DUALITY

What does this duality mean?
The prison of opposites ....
the tensions of in and out,
up and down, good and bad,
love and hate?
Destined to see-saw madly between extremes –
forced to adopt an opinion –
a game to reinforce the ego.

The 'higher third' of Oneness
embraces 'either-or'
transforming them into 'both-and'.
Holding all differences,
comparisons and antagonisms
in one loving embrace.

So waves competing for space
and fighting for their turn to flourish,

**return to the calm deep of the ocean,
recognising not the duality
but the mutuality of all Life.**

"Carpe diem"?   I don't think so!
The day has instead seized us...
Throwing us into a crazy medley
of talking, cooking, driving,
concert-going, thinking, laughing;
and general amazement at the
Magic Show of Life.

Until, exhausted by doing,
we get flopped down on the sofa
to unwind.

Another day – apparently –
in the story of our days;
filling the Eternal Now
with the play of Consciousness.

Quietly now, sleep approaches –
its calm blessing
an interval of peace
before the adventure of tomorrow.

What was your original face
before your grandparents were born?
Was it a mask ... like now?
A 'persona' ... the image
you wish the world to see?

And how did you create this mask?

Who taught you what it should look like?
Your parents, friends, family,
Lovers, neighbours,
Priests or politicians.
Who?

And how do you know if it fits you?
Is it tight – suffocating
the joy and energy
that is your birthright?
Is it loose – so that you can
see around the edges,
and others can see the real You?

And will you finally take it off?
At your last breath or before?

Sensing the nonsense of it …
the deceit of it.

Can you just drop it?

So the world and you
will not be separated.
Barriers will disappear
in the union of Self and Other.
… and laughing,
everyone will enjoy your real smile!

WISDOM

What wisdom is there in words?
Words that divide and separate
Creating concepts and images.

Is wisdom to be found in silence?
... in the holding up of a flower
instead of speaking?

Is it in the perfume of a rose,
the whisper of wind through the trees?
The sweet chattering of birds?

Is it in knowing that consciousness
is not personal – but is the
Pulse of Life in everything?

The hidden knowledge -
the direct seeing - the intuitive insight –
all these are Wisdom ... and more.

Words can only point ...
and at the still centre of the turning world.
the wise quietly smile.

Before the Big Bang

Uncreated worlds brewed in the mind of God.

Imaginings of cosmic games became possibilities;

and, in a wild orgy of creation, became reality.

But of course, there was no 'before', nor 'after';

as time is a dream of humans,

invented to separate two events.
When only one event can be
experienced at any moment –
no other event exists.

There is only This - Here - Now.
The clock stops in this eternal moment.
The moving pen ... the humming computer...
the next thought.

The creation of the universe –
happening in this awareness.
Stepping out of time, this moment becomes
eternal.
The simple bliss of this breath,
Exhaling happiness.

End of summer ...
Brown leaves waving goodbye ...
Silently.

Carousel

There is a loud and brightly
decorated fairground carousel
going round and round.
All those on board are excited
with the ride, shouting:
"We're getting there!"

This goes on and on,
but every now and then
someone wakes up to
what is happening...
and quietly gets off the carousel,
never to be seen again.

Sitting silently in a village church,
Peace settled on us,
as it has settled for a thousand years;
as dust on the stones,
as prayers from the minds
of the millions who
have passed through this place.

Away from the vain striving
of the world outside –
the frustrated demands of
not wanting what we have,
and wanting what we don't have;
the pointless railing against reality.

This place of quiet contemplation
where so many have sought meaning and solace;
connected us to stillness and living calm.
Time slowed ...
until the chill of the stone floor
provoked our departure
into the Autumn rain.

Leaving this ancient sanctuary,
adorned with memorials
of forgotten lives;
an island of peace in a world gone mad.
We take the perfume of silence –
a sacred gift ...
and resume the journey of our lives.

Our universe is one giant recycling factory –
apparent matter collected
and transformed by energy...
a life force that knows no waste;
no birth and no death.

And so we too, appear clad in star dust
to disguise consciousness itself;
sharing air and water with the world.

Until, like leaves turning into soil into trees;
or puddles into clouds into oceans;
we re-appear as something else
- eternally new.

The Game

Is this Life competing against itself?
Striving to win,
exalting in triumph –
anguishing in defeat?

Did love dream up this nightmare of separation...
of seeing all others as rivals or threats?

Yes... and yes – the game is taken seriously
in the game of 'me' –
Unconscious and insane,
we spill sad energy everywhere.

The cure for pain is in the pain;
and when God blows the final whistle;
the game ends –
Players wake up...
and winners and losers all
will fall into each others' arms
and become One.

Autumn leaves fall to feed next year's seedlings;
Connection is all around –
Water and fire ... earth and wind;
Enemies and friends all at once.
No more North and South,
This or that, or good or bad;
See how things blend and connect;
a thrown pebble affects the entire ocean.

Asleep, we pass through one another
Like blowing snow – the known
Merging with the unknown;
Feeling this, there is nothing we have to say.

The world is our reflection, and Love
Glows like a winter fire in our hearts.
We are spirit, light, energy,
Vibration, colour and love –
What more connection can there be?
The magical Oneness of two!

Butterfly

Sweet symbol of eternity – you are what
the caterpillar sees as the end of the world.
You count not months but moments
and yet have time enough to
guarantee your immortality.
You lead us to the sunny side of life –
when, surprising you on a flower,
your gift is a sudden burst of joy.
You represent happiness,
which, when pursued is always
just beyond our grasp.
But if we sit quietly,
it may come to rest on us.
Bees may sip honey from flowers,
and hum their thanks as they leave –
but flowers thank butterflies for their visits.

For you go where you please –
and please wherever you go.

The world is the mirror of awareness –
the purest field of snow
when free of concepts ...
the mind of not-knowing.

In the absence of ego, there is a recognition
of coming home to what we really are;
as the earth accepts its coat of gold,
the autumnal gift from the trees.

Knowing that beyond the grey clouds
of mood and mind, the sun
of liberation always shines in the
pure blue sky of awareness.

Winter approaches, with its damp mornings
and darker evenings -
prompting gloomy mood
and sad memories.

Without the dark there can be no light;
no bliss without misery –
and so the world turns
... the show continues;
the story unfolds until we wake
within the dream.

We are receivers of Life's music.
The symphony is the same
although the sound may differ.

For some the signal is strong and clear;
for others it is weak and suffers from
interference by the mind.

The music is always playing –
the transmission is infinite...
we receivers are impermanent.

We break down, develop faults;
need to be disposed of –
but we are not these things.

We are truly the music, the orchestra,
the conductor and the composer.
We listen, imprisoned in our receivers;
then are liberated to be the creator of all;
to inherit the airwaves.

TV

Television – the opium of the masses,
Inducing the trance of apathy;
where intellect is abandoned
in favour of mindlessness.

The voyeurism of soap operas,
assuming others' lives and dramas;

enables the forgetting of one's
own painful realities.

The filling of mind and
the killing of time...
the escapism from the
emptiness of personal stories.

The identification with celebrity,
life styles and imaginary lives ...
the vacuous substitution
for the real thing.

Until the set is turned off,
and the ensuing silence
drives shrivelled souls to bed.

On the ocean of awareness ... stuff floats.
There's stuff in our heads,
and stuff in our houses.
There's stuff in our hearts,
and in our lives.
Our stories are made of stuff...
Memories, images, attitudes,
Hopes, fears ... all mind stuff.

And the funny thing is –
All this stuff is made of ocean!

The stuff thinks it is an important wave –
permanent and impressive.

It is just water – a ripple
on the surface of the ocean of Life;
lasting simply this moment.

Dive below the surface;
and an immense and infinite stillness,
free from stuff ... awaits us all.
No ... IS us all.

There is a dream of separation;
of personal affairs being organised;
of lives being led.

No more real than a unicorn;
no more useful than a
chocolate teapot.

There is this ... now.
whatever is perceived
happening ... spontaneously.

Say 'Yes' to it all –
allow everything to be
just as it is.

After all, it can't be anything else,
so why declare war
on reality?

Watch the moving energy that you are part of –
feel the love
in everything you are.

There's no time but the present...
no place to go but here.

No-one to be but the Self;
pretending to be you.

No freedom but this breath,
breathing itself.

No love but this light
filling the room.

No music but this silence
in the heart.

No voice but that of Life
calling quietly to Itself.

Whispering the soft words
of truth.

That Life and Love are One ...
and You are That.

Winter passes in misty mornings
and the smell of wet leaves;
Thoughts of summer seem distant memories
and the sun teases with brief appearances.

Days lengthen imperceptibly through
the grey drabness of passing time.
The garden sleeps in decaying damp and cold;
dreaming of warmth and light.

Still the mind busies us with plans
and tasks, filling each day with
agitation and restlessness, demanding
activity and achievement.

Peace lies beyond doing;
outside of any mental activity.
The awareness that contains all
perceptions and plans never changes.
Resting there, without movement,
allowing all things to arise and pass;
We let go, and become Truth.

Experiences come and go ...
we judge them as good, neutral or bad.
The mind accordingly wants 'more',
'better' or 'different' experiences,
and so Life is evaluated with
'shoulds' and should nots'.
Things are as they are –
How could they be different?
Desiring change means rejection of
What Is ... This ... Here ... Now.
Creating a fantasy of the future
Based on dismissing the present,
and memories of the past.

A mind full of concepts creates
systems of belief – networks of
thoughts held to be true.
But thoughts are not facts ...
They are not even real ...
and a life based on belief is a delusion
built on a mirage.

The light of Love shows us the way
If we can see through the mists of ego.
Life will offer its hand to guide us ...
We only need to accept its offer.

Seeking everywhere for answers to mind's questions,
we desire to achieve liberation from looking.
It doesn't occur to us to simply stop.
Dissatisfaction with what is drives us on.

We are already what we are seeking,
but the mind won't accept something
so obvious... so simple ... so easy
as just letting go ... and Being.

Enlightenment must be reserved for
spiritual athletes, the ascetic
who has dedicated years of practice
and renounced the world.
Isn't that the reward for a life of sacrifice?
This breath, nothing more,
holds the key to Truth.
Follow it ... go inwards ... touch what is Real.

Truth is right here ...
behind this thought ...
that concept.
Aware of all experience,
it never changes ...
it awaits its discovery by No-one.

Self is seeking Itself,
enjoying the journey home
from Here to Here.
Fascinated by the scenery and adventures;
amused at the mind's delusions and obsessions;
how ego is distracted by sensations,
seeking happiness in the world,
whilst ignoring the joy available
through turning inward.

Truth is right here, my friends.
Stop searching, striving and expecting.
Be still and allow the Real
to creep up to where you are ...
and surprise you with Love!

Time is a nonsense of the mind.
Now is outside time, and the world is dancing Now
in the eternal present.
Moment by moment everything
is appearing for the first time ... always fresh!
Creation stories are fairy tales
invented by those for whom
Time and Space are real.
What is real never changes
contains all appearances;
all concepts, including time and space.

Here – Now – all is beginningless
and endless.
Startlingly new and unimaginably old.
The first and last...
wrapped in silence.

The photo album lays open,
witness to memories
of past joys ... holidays ..
birthday celebrations; family gatherings.
Evidence of lives of individuals
apparently lived within time.

The illusion of time...
Spinning tales of yesterday,
creating the stories that populate a lifeline.
Filling up a past which fades from our memories
like the disappearing wake of a ship.
The fiction of 'me' ... propped up
convincingly with a history
and biographical details.
All smoke and mirrors
within awareness.
No more real than writing on water.
As captivating as a rainbow,
but just as lacking in substance.

The mind seeks entertainment and stimulation
outside itself;
as if looking within
stokes the fear of emptiness.
Meaning created by perceptions
occupies the intellect, which
searches for concepts and theories
away from the source of All.

Spending time with ourselves,
and turning inwards,
fills our world

with infinite capacity.
Stories, desires, needs and sensations
can all be observed with
a gentle curiosity...
The greatest show on earth!
What need of TV, theatre, shops,
computers, and other toys of the mind?
Stop and look! Reality is Here ...
in the silence of awareness.

The imagination plays with polarities,
creating opposition where none exists;
placing light against dark...
good against evil.

The curse of separation
divides us against each other;
forging differences in the furnace
of opinion and belief...
and in turn feeding fantasies,
suspicions and superstitions.

So the concepts of dark forces
and wicked intent arise ...
sorcery, witchcraft and the evil eye.
abolishing reason with fear.

Beyond the fevered imagination,
the waves on the ocean of Life
continue to rise and fall,
moved by the energy which fills all things;
Is everything ... loves everything.
We forget we are That!

The wonder and joy in young children
is a sign of egolessness ...
a state that is lost
in the rush to adulthood.

Such simplicity can be regained
in later years, as the burdens
of middle age may be laid aside.
So the very young and the lucky old
can share the secret of happiness:
living in this present moment.

Forgetting the burdens of memory,
and letting go all future fantasises;
the magic of being here, now,
is finally recognised.

Children and grandparents share
this fullness of being ...
being one with the flames of a winter's fire;
or one with the blackbird in Spring,
calling for a mate ... just this...
Fresh perceptions for beginners' minds.

All this world is one appearance...
a unified whole.
Any division diminishes it,
creates conflict, comparison, competition,
and war.

Any action affects everything else
in this manifestation.

There are no individuals
making decisions,
although it might seem that way.

All is happening
just the way it has to.
There is no need to worry or resist...
All is well!

Message to a Child.

There are many things you will do
and many things you will have.
Do not value them.
they are impermanent
and meaningless.

Remember how you see the world now;
through beginner's eyes
and an open heart.
No agenda of desiring...
no critical analysis.
Just this ... now...
In all its fresh glory.

Before the programming of separation begins –
promise to yourself that
you will always recall
the connection you now feel to All;
to fly with the birds and flow like the ocean.

A wave has a peak and a trough
but is always the ocean.
Clouds may be grey and thick
but the sky behind remains blue.
There can be no darkness
unless we know light.
Moods come and go
in the awareness that we are.
Grief and hopelessness
give way to smiles of joy.
The deep acceptance of what is
is Love in action.
Tragedies and comedies played out
on a stage ... in a story
told by Life to Itself.

On the other side of belief
the mind falls silent.
Not knowing the way forward
without reliance on the past.

On the other side of concepts
there is only awareness.
No labelling, judging or analysis ...
just spacious openness.

Hating a vacuum, the mind jumps in
with its commentary and criticism;
Nagging at idleness, and pressing for action...
any action to occupy the future
and escape this empty moment.

This moment which contains
all we need ... where identity disappears;
and the mind becomes redundant.
Blue sky, smell of coffee, Handel on the radio,
This perfection ... here ... now.

Cold spring morning
Reading Wei Wu Wei
Listening to Couperin
Drinking coffee....
Nobody.

Rather ... Life unfolding
in all its ways;
here, through the story of graham;
there, through the story of others;
although there is no here or there;
just this ... now.
Energy moving through forms.
Breathing, hearts beating,
Listening, drinking ... all activity
simply happening – to no purpose.
Spontaneously ... the One becomes All.
Dancing the creation of appearances.
Why? Because it can!

There is little to say,
as each word takes us away
from wordless reality, and
pulls us into a world of concepts.
The fairground ride of ideas
that keeps us entertained
and even hypnotised.

Trapped in samsaric dramas,
We forget the simple joys
Of sipping tea, eating cake
and watching birds.

Of course, we don't do these things;
in reality sipping, eating and
watching are just happening.
Electrons and energy are being
displaced spontaneously
and synchronously.

The sleeping fox on the lawn
breathes out as I breathe in ...
the dance of Life!

It's difficult being a person. Not knowing just what you are; but being in no doubt **that** you are. The adventure of being alive unfolding around you ... with no real sense of control. Persuaded that we can choose; have free will; steer our course through the tangled undergrowth of our story. The script unwritten ... the action improvised. Whatever appears to happen to this apparent person has to be

... just the way it is. Allowing everything to be the way it is; trusting Life to be ultimately benevolent ... that all will be well. This is the lesson to be learned.

A fertile emptiness ...
capacity for all and anything;
everything and no-thing can fill it –
no censorship is present.

Right now ... the taste of pepper;
the smell of garlic roasting;
the deep red of a Syrah
with spring sunlight glistening on the glass.
Bach on the radio
and memories all moving through awareness.

Welcoming all - avoiding judgments;
savouring the journey
through the experiences that Life sends.
Not choosing or deciding –
curiosity arises as to what is coming next?

Ageing in mind and body, the diagnoses collect.
The list, boringly negative, lengthens.
As if Life is pushing tolerance
to its limits; the challenges mount.

And yet, the joy underneath
Each experience becomes more apparent.
The sheer miracle of This ...
Happening now ... dominates perception.

The mood rises and falls,
like the weather outside.
Clouds and sunshine compete
for the sky's hospitality.

There is a welcome for all –
Joy, depression, weariness ...
they all parade through awareness.
Just perfection ... just This.

Whispering across the centuries
in images, words and ideas;
Civilisations speak to me.

Once confident of immortality,
Now scattered ruins
and incomplete histories;
their peoples have vanished.

Shadows of belief remain ...
weathered by wars and conflicting dogmas;
the instinctual search for meaning
in a meaningless world.

Too soon wiped out, their prophecies
doomed to eternal doubt ...
a profound silence descends
on the mysteries of their fate.

The quest for truth still agitates the restless mind.
The truth that is simply here, now ...
In the wind rattling the windows.

Imprisoned by a conceptual world created by the mind, we inhabit a phenomenal universe founded on beliefs which are rarely challenged or questioned. Cognition/thinking/mind (*whatever one wishes to call this critical function of objectifying and classifying experience*) divides and labels perceptions; so that a certain smell is labelled 'coffee' a certain taste is called 'strawberry' and so on, through sights, sounds, thoughts and feelings; until all we know are concepts, ideas, images, phenomena. The noumenon is covered up by objects which have been reified ... and do not exist in reality. What a farce!

A prison of perceptions, constantly demanding attention – hijacking awareness – or at least appearing to 'hijack' awareness. In reality Awareness just Is ... it cannot be affected by any object; as it contains and gives rise to all objects. It appears as All. The individual that assumes the role of 'me' is a conceptual construction ... given the illusion of continuity, and of having a past and future, by thoughts/memories/perceptions/ideas. These amount to no 'thing' ... they are simply movements of energy in the vast alive emptiness in which all things are manifest.

All knowledge is constructed, and therefore transient, incomplete, and untrustworthy. Why should ideas be believed? Drop all beliefs, assumptions and opinions ... they are worthless! The construct 'graham' plays the role that appears to be expected of 'him' ... a plausible performance. No one is deciding what to do; no free will is being exercised. Things simply happen ... and the blackbird sings, the tea is drunk, the mind churns out its stream of mental activity ... all in the achingly marvellous and ultimately meaningless dance we call Life.

How did the blackbird come to sing
with the voice of God?
What crazy joy!
What wild improvisations...
that resonate with every living being.

And how did the garden come to glow
with such wonderful new growth?
Startling and surprising the onlooker
with sudden colours and infinite greens.

And does all this majesty
appear in my awareness?
Is all this amazing miracle of life
contained in me?
Can it be true?

If so, then the universe
takes my place; and I make way
for ... and become
All that is.

What is not welcomed
tends to be resisted.
Resistance grows
and suffering appears.

Today the wind is shaking the garden;
flowers and leaves waving
with the energy moving through them.
The mind disapproves.

Unaccepting of what is ...
desire arises for what is not.

Opposing the wind, energy is
expended uselessly.

Flying with the wind ...
stretching our wings with acceptance;
We are lifted up and
away from resistance.

Soaring with the birds,
who are one with the wind;
Exultant with the movement of Life
... ecstatic with simply Being.

Perception leads to conception;
which leads to belief.
... and so life is crystallised
and fragmented.

Letting the impressions and ideas
flow unimpeded,
our stories continue their
mysterious journeys.

Looking on, the witness enjoys
the passing show with
curiosity and equanimity;
Free from identification.

Until the witness, too, disappears;
and all separation fades away;
Leaving only This ...
which is All and No thing.

Hot sunshine, rose petals on the lawn;
Blackbird singing, the perfume of jasmine;
... a moment out of time.

What is this?
Words filling empty space;
trying to reflect reality

Two flies mating on
the sweet pea stem ...
just patterns of energy.

The breeze brushing against my skin,
sensations defined ...
Awareness classified.

The mind doing its job ..
identifying, evaluating,
remembering, speculating.

Behind the mental activity ...
the cognition and recognition;
a sense of peace.

Watching the amazing miracle
of a spider building its web.
Humbled ... the mind falls silent.

The pilgrimage to truth
is the shortest journey –
Turning inwards, we see
there is only This ... Now.

As consciousness is all there is,
where could we go ...
what could we find
that is not self-shiningly
evident right here?

The mind creates the imaginary destination ...
the Shangri-la of dreams;
but the mind is itself a product
of dreaming,
appearing in awareness.

Conscious awareness contains all –
Never changes –
All journeys begin and end here;
and the weary pilgrims discover
they were always Here ... always Home.

The story of our lives is convincingly real. Emotions, thoughts and sensations arise constantly and are entertained and attended to – we feel the 'movie' is reality. It is the ultimate deception ... the cause of all problems and suffering. All inputs are related to a false 'self' and judged accordingly. Desire and aversion are experienced and we are caught in a continuous drama of wanting things to be other than they are.

But things are as they are ... as they need to be ... and are an invitation to us to understand what is real, and what is not real. The very fact that experiences are fleeting and insubstantial should teach us they are not real, and therefore we should not be attached to them. All thoughts, feelings and sensations are temporary disturbances of energy ... and are not who we really are. What we really, *really* are is beyond all these things, beyond concepts, words or thoughts. It is behind and 'upstream' of all ideas or mental activity, and to speak or write about this is impossible.

Nevertheless, when suffering and illusion is witnessed, there arises the impulse to dispel ignorance and to encourage knowledge, where possible. Each movie is different, however, and each journey must be completed in its own way. The message of knowledge may not be heard, and should never be pushed. Those with ears to hear will hear the message.

The powerful illusion of time conditions us to believe that there is some future point where everything will be fine ... enlightenment will occur ... whatever. Enlightenment will not 'occur' to anyone ... it IS. It is not an experience or state to be achieved.

Do you know something?
You are not at all who you think you are!

You are not your body;
You are not your mind.

You were not born;
and neither will you die.

The world was not here before you;
Nor will it exist when you are gone.
You are not in the world,
and neither are you separate from other objects.

You don't agree? Fine!
Just gently inquire … are all your beliefs true?

Consciousness is all there is….
Everything conceived or perceived
appears in, and as, consciousness.

You can use any word you prefer,
instead of consciousness – Awareness, Absolute,
Oneness, Unicity, Christ-consciousness,
Buddha-nature, God … whatever.

Of course, the word is not the thing –
the map is not the territory.
The non-conceptual cannot be conceived.
The ineffable cannot be described.
It contains all … is all.
Nothing more can be said.

We appear in It, as an expression of Itself.
Being lived, we lose ourselves
in our stories and identities,
imagining we are in control.
Thinking that we are making
choices ... what a joke!

**Autumn leaves ...
do they know
what happened?**

If you think you have done something today...
Think again!
Nobody did anything.
Things were done; but no-one did them.
Actions happened, but no actor was involved.
Events unfolded, and the programmed
and conditioned organism which
you may call 'you', appeared to perform
actions and make choices.
Consciousness held all activities
and assumed all roles in this
miraculous performance.
Really knowing this ...
seeing through the illusion of self-hood ...
is truly liberation.
Of course, things happen;
but not the way you think.
Whatever you believe you've done - you didn't.
Whatever you think you've achieved – you haven't.
Whatever mistakes you think you made – you didn't.
Sure ... things appeared to happen
in the story you call your life;

but you did not do any of them.
Because there is no 'you'.
If you don't believe me, try to find yourself.
Wherever you search, there is only consciousness …
An awareness that knows that all there is …
including any 'personal' fictions,
is here … now… and is totally perfect.

Is it the rushing of the wind
over the treetops?
Or the pulsing of blood cells
Through our capillaries?

Is it the trembling bees
on the swaying buddleia?
Or the miraculous movement
of stars in the night sky?

The surprising power of living things
to be themselves … to become
What they are destined to be.
Thoughts are swept through awareness
by this force … sometimes
with the extra impetus of emotions.

This, all this movement …
is Life expressing itself;
from the smallest sprouting seed,
to the heaving oceans.
There is no separation in the Dance of
Becoming.

I have no idea what's going on.
I can't trust any so-called knowledge
to be absolute truth …
it's all relative and conditional …
and therefore not Real in any sense.

I won't trust it any more…
or anything else my senses or mind present
within consciousness.
Concepts ... percepts ... they come and go.
I can't imagine what it all means.

… so I have stopped imagining.
Stopped believing anything …
Even in the story of 'graham'.
It is a meaningless role that genetic programming
and social conditioning has created.
A script that is followed.
It happens when needed ... on some kind of auto-pilot.

I watch it, amused, impartial … not expecting or
needing any results.

The day begins; things get done …
The mind sorts stuff and seems to prioritise,
respond and make decisions.
But no-one is deciding ... or in control;
No-one is at home.

The day ends; appetites are fed … needs are met;
the body finds its own equilibrium.
No-one has done anything.
Yet nothing is left undone.

What kind of strange performance is this ...
Without a performer?
A play without actors ...
A game without players?

Still the watching continues, intermittently;
Silent ... impartial ... impersonal.
Loving ... being Love ... Being.
Just This ... aaaah!

Raging against reality...
Arguing with 'what is' ...
We are simply re-arranging
the furniture in our prison cell.
Unaware that the door stands open,
we choose not to leave the comfort
of our illusory world.
Electing instead to lose ourselves
in the duality of appearances.

Not really losing, but re-creating
ourselves in the image of our imagination -
the portrait created by thought and memory.

As separate entities, we seem to move
in and out of others' lives;
Suffering loss, grief, remorse and the range of emotions
fed by thoughts which are believed.
Meanwhile, out at sea, the waves
dance and revel in their unity of apparent differences.

The music of 'our lives'...
a symphonic study ...
both harmonious and dissonant;
stormy and peaceful.

Patterns of energy moving into a song of Life ...
The sound of the wind
through the willow trees in the Spring;
and the crashing of waves on a wintry beach.

The blackbird's liquid beauty,
The jackdaw's raucous shout ...
all are part of this composition;
All have their place,
Balancing soft with hard –
Pianissimo with fortissimo –
Adagio with allegro.

Until our music fades;
and the notes which formed our story
disappear into the Silence
from which they came.

Needing to keep busy ...

Mind producing tasks ...

Can't I just look out the window?

There is a lightness in Being
that requires no effort;
The universe is served up
within the awareness of You.

The luxury of breathing in ... aaah!
The warmth of sunlight on the skin;
Smells, sounds, sights ...
arriving here ... now...
as a feast of perceptions.

Concepts, memories, ideas ...
all these appear too;
Inviting attention (sometime demanding it);
but moving through and leaving no trace...
as waves on the ocean of experience.

All is taken care of ... actions occur – or not;
Things happen, and may be judged
as good or bad – or not;
Letting go – Life lives Itself.

Underneath the neighbour's gutter,
a butterfly caught in a spider's web.
Struggling in vain, it becomes
more entangled in its captor's silken trap.

The spider watches patiently,
making brief and hurried forays
to reinforce its web,
waiting for its dinner.

The butterfly flails furiously ...
pitifully ... not complying

with its inexorable fate;
fighting against the dying of its light.

It did not plan to end this way ...
enjoying the buddleia, just feet away;
feeling the August sunshine,
warming its wings;
just moments ago.

Perhaps it had laid its eggs
on the cabbage leaves;
and its function was fulfilled ...
its offspring guaranteed?

We do not know these things ...
just that now it hangs there,
flapping its captive wings
in protest at its lost freedom.

The spider moves in at last,
delivering its venomous 'coup de grace'.
The struggling slows down ... ceases.
Energy is transferred from one form to another.

The silhouette of tattered wings is still;
the spider, sated,
retires into its dark home...
and night draws near.

No mourning; no grief; no funeral rites,
just a transformation ...
a shift of energy
in the dance we call Life.

Words appearing from emptiness
scattering meaning across the page ...
recalling another day that
appeared in awareness ... Now
... and now is gone.

The transience of existence
showing in the untidy garden
exhausted by the labours
of summer growth.

The spectacle fading like the warmth
of the September sun.
The quiet, gentle decay into the earth ...
preparing the cover for the cold to come;
the hibernation of seeds and bulbs
which promises new birth and fresh life.

Another Autumn ...
the year turning towards its end ...
and a breathing out of fruitfulness.

Growing Old

The stories of lives unfold
over the apparent years ...
in the space called Now;
and so the memories seem more real
than the feared futures.

The real and imagined separations ...
of loved ones, friends, identities;
All disappearing into the
vagueness of past regrets.

Do these 'elderly', labelled
by an uncaring world,
realise their new identity,
their role as 'burdens on society'?

Or in their distant memories,
do they relive their youthful adventures;
their romantic mistakes ...
escaping the present realities?

Waiting for cancer, coronary or confusion ...
the old feel the cold.

All separations are illusions.
There is only this moment
containing eternity;
Until the mind jumps in and divides ...
Young and old, good and bad;
... and so on and on.

We live in separation ... our sense of self
a badge of loneliness which we
foolishly nurture and protect.
The divisions are false ... the walls
between us simply a mirage.

Be still ... in this eternal moment
All is present ... in unity.
Time and space are realised
as mere concepts ... tools used to separate.
This breath ... this heartbeat ....
Is enough to hold the universe.

Like thirsty fish,
we search for what is
in and all around us.
We seek to become what
we already are ... and claim it as 'ours'.

The next teacher, book, group
or meeting will help us
become the person we want to be.
We just need to silence our minds;
find our 'inner selves';
abandon all desires;
cleanse our unconscious;
and balance our chakras.

Then, in time, we will be liberated.
What tosh! The only prison is the one
we make for ourselves ...
with our concepts and beliefs.
The enlightenment dream keeps us asleep;
and the ego's subtle games
maintain the fundamental mistake of dualism.

Stop! Right here is all you need.
Perfection hidden in appearance.
All that is ... manifest in this moment.
Let the mind divide and judge
... that's what it does.

The robin's song from the holly tree –
The tired limbs resting in the chair –
The taste of a good cabernet sauvignon –
This ... and then This. Now.
... barely disguised perfection!

All we ever need is appearing before us.
Let go of thoughts and beliefs
... and feast on the banquet of Life!

The illusion of free will
implies freedom of thought
and the exercise of control over one's destiny.

Let's examine these assumptions:

Firstly, the concepts of free will, control and destiny are simply that –
Concepts made of thoughts.   What is thought?

Not something under your control,
I would suggest.
What will your next thought be? Don't know?
Then you have no control.
If you did, why would you choose to have unhappy thoughts?
Wouldn't you select only happy thoughts and live in a state of perpetual happiness?

So let's be quite clear about this -
Thinking just happens. We have no idea what we will think ... the pattern of energy simply appears in awareness ... and then disappears. Sometimes a thought carries an emotional 'charge'; and feelings (together with bodily sensations) arise to strengthen that thought. Positive and negative emotions both

delay the thought's disappearance;
sometimes for minutes and hours
of sentimental reflection.
There is nothing special or mystical about any
thought - it is just an impulse of energy –
a fart of the brain ...
a puff of inconsequential and
spontaneous psychic air!

So ... let them all go ... rest in Awareness!

Not a 'thing' ... not a concept or an idea, image or
thought –
before all these ... YOU ARE.
Closer than your skin,
nearer than your breath;
more intimate than any whirling atom which
dances your body into existence.

Without beginning or end ...
birth or death;
before time and outside space,
You and I ARE.

All divisions collapse into unity...
into Oneness, and then less than that;
the absence of presence **and**
the non-absence of presence.
All paradoxes and contradictions
are included/excluded
in this marvellous and awful beauty
that WE ARE.

Before the conceptual explanation
I have no idea how breathing happens,
but it simply happens.
Food is digesting,
Blood is circulating,
Cells are dying and dividing.
I have no idea why ....
or who is doing all this.
It simply is happening.

Thinking is happening too ...
why should I assume
I am doing this?
Sure, things are happening –
this pen is writing on this page;
the sun is shining;
birds are singing.

Coffee will be made and drunk;
biscuits will be eaten –
plans will be made; worries worried –
pain felt – all the perceptions and emotions
that arise will be experienced -
by whom?

I look for the 'me' who experiences ...
as I have searched for decades – and find no-one.
There's nobody at home.
Just a story of a character in a drama;
a narrative comprising slices of memory,
... snapshots of a 'life'.

Of course, it seems that this body-mind
has been conditioned by genes and experience.
There are likes, preferences, opinions, values –

all the trappings of a person...
the baggage of biography.
But
There's no actor in the costume –
No face behind the mask.

Plagued by darkness
I escape into the light ...
Distractions have their uses
when oblivion threatens
to eclipse both mood and action.

To the shops ... to see human activity
and interaction; to play the game
half-heartedly –
Going through the habitual motions.

When will this charade end?
The pretence of being separate ...
this theatre of the absurd.
I've had enough.

Knowing in my heart that there is no do-er,
I remain busy doing.
The apparent man living an apparent life ...
until his apparent death.

Is it time to write?
The pen is moving across the page ...
words are appearing.
Searching for the writer reveals nothing –
No-one at home ... again.
It seems that the force that moves

planets around the universe
has chosen to write.

Communicating with itself, it is
teasing consciousness with concepts.
Ideas bubbling up from the depths
emerge in new forms and meanings;
Unsought, spontaneous ...
Life scribbles its stories to entertain Itself.

So writing happens ...
accompanied by a soundscape -
rain falling against the window;
the sound of Russian from the kitchen,
the intimate rushing of tinnitus ...
whispering a loving 'hush' of Now.

The Sunday routine is under way,
dancing with the mirage of time;
Filling the day with activity
that appears to be planned.

Thoughts and actions spill over each other
in random and habitual patterns;
and we go about our lives content
under the illusion of control.

This ... now ... the humming of the boiler,
The running and shouts of children next door ...
Life is appearing in awareness.
This is enough ... but the mind wants more.

One more day in the calendar of our lives;
dull with habit and tired with effort.

Do we have to play this game?
Must we keep up the pretence?

Soon will be time for coffee ...
the ironing and garden pruning awaits.
Things will be done – by no-one.

May we ask for less
and offer more.
Leaving behind desire and dissatisfaction,
may we cherish sweet simplicity.
The opportunity to be here ... with this breath;
in this moment.

Sensing all that is available
to senses that open ...
and may the seeing contain no 'see-er';
may the hearing harbour no 'hearer';
the touching no 'touch-er' ....
May tasting and smelling possess no subject...
and may thinking hide no thinker.
May we be simply here ... it is enough.

It's all been said very well before ...
Enlightenment (so-called) is the
extinction of the very self that
is searching for enlightenment.
Hence the impasse.

The self is required for seeking,
so why not call off the search?
Then the self (*cunning bastard!*) will be

pretending not to search ...
trying not to try ...
seeking not to seek.

Until ... paralysed by its own *koan*,
it may give up – simply stop.
And as in the shipping forecast,
It may "slowly lose its identity".

So, unlooked for ... uninvited;
Peace may arise.
The self is exposed for the fraud it is;
and the awareness that we truly are
is simply All That Is.

The head is full of too much –
too many memories, ideas,
concepts and facts.
All these feed the mind,
enabling it to label and
evaluate experience.
Dividing and judging ...
and ultimately wanting
things to be different.

This pervasive dissatisfaction
sours the moment,
and creates the fantasy
of future happiness.

Happiness is This ...
stopping to listen to Mozart,
accompanied by the kettle in the kitchen;
the smell of fresh coffee;

The taste of panettone ...
happiness is the simple miracle
of Being – here – now.
... what more could be desired?!

Surprised by sunshine,
a January Sunday
blinks, bemused,
over the garden.

Fooled by warmth,
spring bulbs,
both shy and bold,
push into the light.

Jackdaws, in clouds of
black crosses,
wheel across the sky
in purposeless joy.

... and a solitary robin
warming up his voice,
stakes his claim
to the viburnum.

This, then, is winter's trick;
tempting us out of the house
to tidy up the memories
of last summer;
deluding ourselves that Spring has come early.

Maybe it has, or perhaps
the icy hand of February awaits;
ready to pounce on

unsuspecting jumper-wearers.

A fresh round of colds and flu –
sniffing and coughing misery
to take us through to
a new and truer season.

Safer to stay indoors?
Avoiding the risk of chills?
No! Let's don our coats and scarves ...
Grab our gloves and secateurs!

The garden awaits its manicure ...
patient, half-awake – watching
the premature sun sink
into early darkness ...
and a more appropriate cold.

Stormy day –
Wind shouting at the windows ...
Who's listening?

What is writing this?
The movement of the pen
can be explained ...
but where do the thoughts come from?
Does anyone own them?

This moment ... and the next.
This breath ... and the next.
Together ... living now.
No thoughts needed!

Bach on the radio –

strangely wonderful listening ...
again no thoughts needed.

But the mind intrudes –
labelling and evaluating
- needlessly.

Another day is nearing its end ...
The baggage of sensations,
Thoughts and feelings
Have been carried around
and tidied away.

Sitting back, in front of a log fire,
Watching flames sputter into life
and disappear
just as quickly.

All is change ... nothing is stable
or permanent;
Just energy adopting
its many appearances ..
feigning reality.

Everything coming and going
in the silent space
of awareness;
that is what we all are –
That is Life.

Nothing but perceptions to build a world and a self;
Imagination creating illusions.
Look inside.
There's no one home!
Objects appear in consciousness
Consciousness appears in awareness;
and All is empty
and All is One.

Why do we believe this dream?
Dividing, labelling, judging.
Thoughts are not real,
nor feelings or sensations.
Yet we are caught up in dramas and fictions;
defending our false egos
and constructing the stories of 'our lives'.
Stop - and see the emptiness behind it all;
the miraculous Suchness of this!

As a passer-by *(as Jesus suggested)*
I notice many things
... or rather, noticing happens.
Notice that past and future don't exist;
that memories and plans are
mere thoughts that need not be believed.

Notice that it is always and only Now;
and that fresh frog spawn
is warming in Spring sunshine.

Notice what is noticing;
the open, limitless and silent space
of awareness ... containing all ...
rejecting nothing.

Notice that here – now ... all is OK
better than OK ... perfect!
no need for more words,
or more dualistic thinking
- just BE.

Don't spend a lifetime looking for happiness
in all the wrong places.
Stop seeking satisfaction from 'outside'.
Look inwards to what is looking.
Feel the humming aliveness of Being.
Notice the certainty of 'I am';
the knowing of awareness
that contains all appearances.

Allow the appearances to come and go
in the soap opera you call your life.
Your story is just a plausible dream.
Happiness is here... now ...
in the quiet miracle of **This**.

In this wild and tragically
tumultuous beauty of living ...
Seemingly thrown to and fro by fickle fate ....
we seem to exist.
Pretending to control events ...
assuming the power of choice;
we foolishly adopt the arrogance
of a subject in control of objects.

In ignorance 'we' construct the narratives
we call our 'lives';

whilst in reality Life is
just spontaneously happening –
without purpose or plan.

Can we drop the intellectualising?
The conceptual theorising?
and be still ...
whilst Life flows.

Life flows continuously –
escaping from the impossible present;
recreating experience afresh in every instant.
And yet the brain applies the brakes
to this natural movement;
demanding answers to incessant questions.

What's that noise? – a pigeon.
What's that movement? – a butterfly.
What's that sensation? – the sun's warmth.
What's that taste, smell, memory, idea ? ...
and so on, in endless interrogation and labelling of Life.

Until we rest – letting all things
arise and depart in silent observation.
Letting go of all concepts and judgments.
Falling silent and simply following
the magical unfolding of this moment,
and the next ....
in this totally miraculous Now!

There's no need to do anything ...
thoughts come unbidden –
perceptions arise unsought.

Just as quickly, they depart, leaving what?
Reactions, ... memories... responses
which are usually automatic ...
born from long-held habits.

If the parade of experiences
is simply observed ...
allowing and letting go;
without attachment or reaction,
no trace is left behind.

The wake of a ship opens up
and closes again,
leaving the ocean untouched.

So let our lives entertain us
from moment to moment;
within the still witnessing of Now.

There's nothing you can do
To get from here to here;
No other place to be except here;
No other time to be except now.

Where or when else could you go?
This is all there is –
Unfolding spontaneously in this moment.
This is as good as it gets!

All seeking can be dropped ...
Let go of 'getting somewhere'.
The waves come to realise
They are nothing but ocean.

Whatever thoughts arise and pass away
Are not yours – they simply happen;
Along with all sensations and perceptions.
You are not doing these things.

Sit back – enjoy the show;
Soon it will be time for sleep,
and the start of other dreams.

The body feels heavy and sluggish;
The skin looks surprisingly old;
Pulsing tinnitus is the 'leitmotif'
of my advancing years.

Yet in this eternal Now,
nothing ages ...
all is refreshingly new...
simply alive.

When this dream of consciousness ends,
as all stories must ...
What stays?
Will there be another Spring like this one?
With more frog-spawn, birdsong,
and joyous daffodils?

Or will this all disappear into
that good night ...

To rest a while before
another production opens ....
on another stage?

Today would be a good day to die.
I have heard all the music
I want to hear ...
Before my ears fail totally.

I have seen all the Springs ...
So many more than my son did.
I have tasted all the foods
and enjoyed all the wines.

Is there more to do?
Cleaning and tidying the house
and garden perhaps?...
but the clutter just returns.

Is there anyone to die?
Certainly there's a story
which must have an end.
The final act of the play.

Will it be soon?
It will still be Now ...
whenever the last breath arrives;
and the wave slips back into the ocean.

Another apparent day to fill with activity. Choices appearing in awareness ... decisions ... actions ... consequences. Apparent causation in a relative world ... and in the Absolute - nothing ever happened. Because no 'thing' exists; just the spontaneous happening of Life. God's dancing Her own entertainment.

What we perceive as 'things' - sensations, thoughts, feelings; are just images flashing through consciousness ... signifying nothing. No real need to plan ... things seem to occur unplanned ... as needed or not. Stuff gets done ... shopping, cooking, eating - the whole show.

I watch, knowing there is no 'I' ... just God watching, waiting for the remembering that we are already Home.

I AM — and because of this
the world IS.
The ten thousand things
appear in me;
and are named by the mind.

The mind labels itself as 'me'
and so a story is born;
the tale of a life that
appears in the world that I AM.

Memories, opinions, preferences .... stuff -

All appears in the mind
that tries to organise life ...
and continuously fails.

I ... you ... we ... are the Life
that tries to see itself ...
Seeks to awaken itself ...
Can we get out of the way?
Can we be still ... and let it flow?
Blackbird singing in evening light ...
what more could be needed?!

The greatest Truth lies behind the mind;
upstream of all thought and perception.
That which contains all experiences
is what you really are.

There is no need to go anywhere,
do anything, wait any time.
You are already what you seek;
you are already home.

Once this is seen, there is only
this blackbird, this symphony;
this now ... and again now ...
unfolding in a miracle of spontaneity.

Looking for causes in the mind;
working out a theory or explanation?
You will be wasting your energies.
Everything is causeless, and in
Reality ... there are no things!

Just the magnificent Nowness of all,
of Nothing appearing as Everything.
Perceptions, like the weather,
pass through ... nothing stays.

Even memories, those
hardened signals from the past,
fade ... gently erasing the pains,
the triumphs, of an imagined yesterday.

Turning Velcro into Teflon,
the mind learns to let go;
facing this amazing moment
in newly born freshness,
and flowing with the
spontaneous dance of Life.

This is as good as it gets ...
there is no tomorrow;
no point in planning.
Everything is taken care of
in order that caring
can give way to living!

Does it know it should be green?
... the old grass,
turning brown.

Easter Sunday, 2014

Another year... another Easter;
This time raining and grey.
Books, music, meditation ...
The usual trappings of graham's story.

An apparent individual
With history, preferences,
Knowledge ... the usual stuff
That clogs up the flow of life.

One act follows another,
Choices seemingly made ..
A succession of perceptions
Threaded together into a day.

This charade will continue
Until its apparent finale;
The last thought ushering in
The final struggling breath.

Until 'then' ... just Handel and chocolate!

Perhaps today is my last?
There will be no raging against
the dying of the light ...
but a glad acceptance
of going into that good night.

Letting go of plans and worries ...

leaving behind aches, pains
and a body that is wearing out.

Quitting a world gone mad
with greed and separation.
No ego left to defend ...
What relief!

Let the flames consume what's left;
and allow the consciousness to slip
into the silent ocean of awareness.
Coming home at last.

All appears in consciousness ...
the body is such an appearance
and because of the senses
the world arises.

Manifestation is dependent on consciousness.
When it disappears, as in
deep dreamless sleep,
the body and the world
cease to exist.

No thing truly exists ...
All objects require consciousness
to be aware of them;
and are therefore
dependent and conditioned.

Look for the real ...
beyond what appears to exist.
Rest in the primordial silence

from which this rich
imagined spectacle arises.

Seven billion snowflakes,
each one uniquely different;
taking its own journey
through time and space.

Imagined separation
evaporating in the
light of wisdom,
and melting into Oneness.

So the drops slip into
the ocean of Awareness,
coming home to the
One taste of the Absolute.

Simply seeing through
the apparent differences,
and the 'selves' that mind creates,
.... This is enlightenment.

No-one becoming Everything
in a watery Paradise!

Nobody home!
No-one was ever home;
but the long-running
soap opera continues.

The stage is populated
by characters imagined and imaginary;

following scripts and improvising
in a crazed exhibition of egomania.

All action happens Now,
informed by an imagined
past and future.

This is all there is,
but judgment wants better;
bigger, different, more
exciting entertainment.

In the absence of the critic,
the play unfolds gently,
flowing through and into Life.

**The smell of washing
hung out to dry ...
time to rest.**

Be still ... there is no need to move;
no need to go anywhere but here;
and no time to be but now.

Everything you seek is just here ...
appearing as this ... and this ...
all you ever sought has always been here.

Nearer than your breath;
closer than your most private thought;
the prize is already won.

Maybe your mask is slipping?
Perhaps your real face is showing
behind the assumed identity?

Just stop ... let go of all pretence;
release those beliefs,
and the burden of ancient
perceptions and meanings.

Be free of all concepts,
and come home to the absolute
simplicity and wonder of who you are!

Is the mind dictating the words
to the writing fingers?
Or are the ideas simply expressing
themselves as movement?

Is there an intellect working as
an intermediary between
Awareness and perceived product?

Or is there no causal relationship...
simply phenomena happening?
Independent of origination ...
a spontaneous appearance?

Sliding home ... nothing to do,
because there is no possible 'do-er'...
no subject to choose or to act.

Home is already This ...
the concepts of 'going', 'arriving',
or 'achieving' are mistakes;
infantile assumptions that
need to be challenged.

Dappled sunlight dancing on the page;
chasing the words as they form
and skip in and out of the shade.

Noises drifting into the garden ...
machinery, drilling, hammering ...
what drives us to work?
To desire results .. the rejection
of what is here; in search of a
better future ... bigger house ...
happier life?

All we need is here ...
and all we need to do
to have all we want ...
is to STOP.

Stop desiring reality to be different –
Stop expecting the world
to give what you want –
Stop wanting what you don't have -
Stop rejecting what you do have –
Simply STOP ... and breathe!

In the spiritual desert which is
the world today ... many mirages appear.

They promise health, wealth and happiness
in their illusory attraction.

The perfect body, the ideal partner,
the best job, the biggest house and car;
all the ingredients of a successful life
are displayed in detail.

And like mesmerised window-shoppers,
we mistake appearances for reality;
beliefs for truth,
and competing for living.

We can stop chasing mirages ...
cease the continual disillusionment
that shatters hopes and dreams.

Look, here, in the oasis that is your heart;
Here is all the joy and peace
that life can offer.

Here is the world;
contained in this moment and this place ...
where the desert is transformed
into wild and fertile beauty,
and a new Eden appears.

Love is a noun, not a verb.
You or I cannot love ...
We **are** love.

Love cannot be gained or given,
Lost or won;
It is our birthright;
Our true nature.

When self gets out of the way,
Love can shine.
When we stop looking for it,
or holding onto it,
Love emerges in everything.

The fly, sitting on my arm
and wringing its hands ...
Is Love.

The breeze, moving the grasses
in the warm sunlight ...
All ... ALL ...
Is Love!

Today everything's heavy!
All seems an effort ...
My meat-suit is tired.
Muscles and bones complain
of having to move ...
Mind is sluggish and jaded.

Yet it is still completely perfect ...
just this aching sleepiness,
is all that needs to be here.
No aims, plans or frustrations ...
just an allowing; a welcoming
of all that appears.

Behind the role;
the false identity ...
a wonderful emptiness.
Capacity for whatever the day
finds to throw into it ...
a happy dustbin!

Soon, a cup of tea with something 'naughty',
perhaps a nap ... perhaps not.
Whatever happens is just fine!

Please understand ... ALL IS ONE! There is absolutely **no separation**. This means that the movement of the air in and out of your lungs is the same as the wind howling through the Antarctic ... the atomic particles making up your body are affected by a movement of neutrons in a distant exploding star. This is one universal dance that we are part of ... there's not even a 'we' that is in any way detached from this fantastic performance. Forget all about an individual with choice and a life to lead ... that's simply a story. Rest in awareness of this breath; this thought; this moment ... of Life unfolding just the way it needs to ... right now!

Lighter today, the mind turns within
to seek the 'do-er' of actions ...
and finds – no thing!

So who was born on 19.5.1951?
Who has lived through
all those experiences?
Who has all this 'knowledge'?

Let's not mix the absolute
with the relative.
Satya with *mithya*.
One contains the other ...
is the other.
There is no ultimate separation.

So 'I' look from behind
the organism called graham ...
see the entity as if seated
in the cinema,
watching the movie unfold,
imagining it is acting,
deciding and controlling ...
but the script is written here,
Now – in the vertical reality
of time and space.

Observing the actor creates understanding,
and the illusory shadow
is dispelled by the
light of insight.

True seeing, interrupted by
the demands of an apparent 'ego',
is always present, taking in

all things, allowing their transience,
and renouncing beliefs and concepts.

Let us relax into this insight,
this wordless/thoughtless knowing.
All is happening as it should,
whether there's an identification
with an imaginary person, or not.
All is well.

Words, words ...
More bloody useless words!
What use is explanation in dualist language?
Where can the imagination venture,
apart from conceptual paths?
How can mere words open
the door to the Deathless?
Why waste time with scribbling?

Perhaps because I want these pages filled?
... or maybe, just maybe...
words can push the door a little;
challenge assumptions;
unpack and question beliefs.

Ask unanswerable questions ...
raise doubts; shake certainties;
undermine dogma, and
annihilate opinions.

So I will continue to write;
though no-one is writing –
Life is scribbling to Itself!

Again and again, words fail ...
their dualist prison is unable to
break free from distinction,
judgment and division.

The whole world seems divided against itself;
given to conflict, greed and delusion.
War, hatred and grief are everywhere
on TV and in the press.
It is so depressing, and the desire
for oblivion is met each night
in the surrender to sweet sleep.

Waking to another day ...
another collection of emotions and experiences.
When will be enough?
When will the journey be over?
What further lessons must be learned?

Perhaps each day offers opportunities
to help ease suffering?
Accomplishing this, I leave
the snail on the garden path.

Conditioning and programming
take care of all actions,
and apparent decisions.
Nothing is personal; just this inevitable
coming together of circumstances
and universal forces ...
to produce This.

Music, writing, aching knee,
tinnitus, taste of melon,
comfort/discomfort, judging.
Everything just happening ...
appearing and disappearing
effortlessly, meaninglessly.
The mind jumps in ... analyses;
compares; evaluates ... as it does.
.... and the fly buzzes in the window
in a vain attempt to reach
the open blue sky beyond.

Watching the news ....
war, conflict, division —
the catalogue of mankind's
unkindness to itself is continuous and
seemingly devoid of hope.

When will the stupidity stop?
Will we ever realise the
indivisible Oneness that
we all share? .... are!
Two sides of the same coin
cannot divorce each other.

We belong to each other,
and in order to survive,
need to recognise
the lack of separation
in all we seem to be.
Just This - only Now -
there is nothing to keep us
from one another.

What happens when the stimulation ends?
... when the smart phones
stop inducing stupidity.
... when TV programmes
cease to numb the brain
with inane drivel.
... when advertising campaigns
drop their endless nagging.
Can we survive the quietness?

Can we cope with simply
Being with ourselves?
... without the ceaseless noise,
the pressure to 'connect',
the constant distractions
that keep us from
simple awareness of This.

Can we learn again to love silence?
... to sit and watch each moment
appear and disappear
in the fullness and peace of Now.

Watching the TV news ...

and the world's madness ...

it's time for a cup of tea.

Trainspotting

Watching ... standing on the platform
as the trains of thought
arrive and depart.
Journeys into the past or future;
inviting us to become
passengers in time.

Remaining on the platform,
trains come and go;
old and new; long and short;
clean and dirty ...
the destinations always uncertain.

Staying here, and declining
the temptation to travel ...
I come to my senses.
The ground under my feet,
the wind on my face,
the sounds and smells of the station,
all fill my awareness ...
Why move away from This?

Driving or Driven?

Gripping the steering wheel tightly,
we steer an apparent course
through the maze of 'our lives'.
Unaware that there is no link
between our desperate manoeuvres
and where we actually go;
we believe we are in control.

There is no-one to control,
and no choice of destiny.
Everything just happens ...
perfectly ... spontaneously;
without a plan or reason.

So perhaps we can let go
of the imaginary steering wheel;
and coast down the freeway of Life?
Less of a driver ... more a passenger;
enjoying the view,
relishing what is experienced ...
in one joyous ride of freedom!

In September sunshine ...
fading flowers
dream of summer.

The screen of awareness holds many images;
appearing as perceptions and conceptions.
All are transient phenomena ...
trees, flowers, bodies ...
physical stuff;
Sensed through eyes, ears, nose,
tongue and skin. ...
Perceived where?

Not in the dark wetness of the cerebrum ...
the 2lb of tofu packed with neurones.
Where else?

On the screen of awareness ...
the windscreen so wide and clear
that nothing escapes it.
The whiteboard of Life!
Infinite ... spotless ... welcoming.

Embracing not just physical objects
but also mental phenomena ... ideas, memories, concepts,
opinions, preferences, emotions ...
again – all transient, temporary and empty.
A passing sideshow of imagining;
seen by no-one.

Who sees? Who thinks? Who knows?
No seer ... nothing seen ... simply seeing.
Just thinking? Just knowing?
Is it that simple?

The sense of being 'lived' continues ...
the pen moves across the page;
the words appear.
Is there meaning beyond the scribbles?

There's no-one to say ... just the
Ocean of experiencing
moving through awareness,
waving, crashing, whispering
the wordless rhythm of Being.

My world cracked open in 2000 ...
that's how the light flooded in.
Separating identity from reality;
image from truth.

The story fell away,
leaving each day a fresh beginning....
a flowing with life.

Now, with little left to act out,
few lines to learn;
the performance moves easily
towards the final curtain.

Sliding home,
more Teflon than Velcro;
the path is easy,
without expectations.

Not looking beyond this ... here ...
the whispering of tinnitus and Delius
in the duet of Oneness.

The Old Elm Tree

One leafy branch prematurely brown;
does this announce your death warrant?

Eighty years you have stood outside;
resisting winter storms;
even the '87 hurricane;
filling the garden with your

Winter leaves, and
pushing up the pavement
in brute shows of strength.

Nesting birds hidden in your arms
despoiled my cars beneath.
You watched many enter and leave ...
both alive and dead.

Now something microscopic
has infiltrated your defences,
and poisons your heart.

It may take time for the canker
to spread in all your veins,
but the end is certain.

I often wondered who would go first ...
you or me.
Now your withered
leaves betray your fate;
the contest may soon be over.

There are no phenomena;
as there is neither time nor space
for any to exist within.

There is simply perceiving ...
seeing the bamboo waving in the garden ...
the clouds drifting across the sky.

The pulsing water-wheel inside my head ...
the stream of thoughts
appearing ... disappearing.

No things ... no objects ...
just a living energy
moving through form.

Purpose, ambition, meaning ...
all lost in the momentum
of Now ... always arriving
with this breath ...
this Love.

**The body may be active or still.
Let it be as it is.**

**The mind may be busy or quiet.
Let it be as it is.**

**Neither is what one is.
Why respond?
Why react?
Let it all be ...
Let it all go ....**

**and let in the pure Joy
that is waiting to
light up our lives.**

A windy autumn afternoon ....
with tea and Beethoven
and a teacake.
What more is needed?

The mind looks for more ...
asks impossible questions ...
unsettles the mood
with expectations and
vague dissatisfactions.

It will be ignored ...
this is all that's needed –
this is all perfect as it is.

Questions can blow away in the wind,
disappearing from the
screen of awareness
as soon as they appear.

Awareness is left alone,
immaculate, untouchable as ever;
holding this one amazing Now.

What is it that we all want?
Happiness? Health? Wealth?
Fame? Status? Power?

Fine then ... spend your lives
Searching after all these ...
Catching and trying to hold
onto any of them.

But first, pause ... before you
spend all that energy.
Consider which of these six
are in any way permanent.
Do they not all change?
Can they be captured and held?
Are they not like the mist at dawn? ...
destined to fade and disappear ...
perhaps to reappear unbidden ... or not?
Is it better then, to seek what doesn't change?
What is outside Time; forever present ...
What is outside Space; always here ....
Stop searching ... it's just This!

The Love that we truly are
is hidden behind the walls of self.
The protection imagined
by the ego is maintained
through a programmed personality.
Carving up life into experiences,
moods, events and situations;
each carefully labelled and managed.

Judging each moment as
acceptable or not ...
satisfying or not ...
and even when accepted,
possession and permanence are sought.
Letting be and letting go
are all the skills we need.

Autumn heralds the ending of
another apparent year in
this apparent 'life' of mine.

Moving through form, energy assumes
many shapes and appears
as impossibly diverse phenomena.

And this energy is what?
Life, Love, God, Brahman?
... all names – all useless.

Mind and its words
cannot capture what is
holding everything;
cannot see the screen
on which all appear.

But relaxing into this breath ...
appreciating all that being alive offers ...
the pleasures and the pains ...
words fade into silent, shining awareness.

The story so far ....
born ...
educated ....
conditioned and socialised.
The result – a spiritual cul-de-sac.
No way out through the mind...
this mind that is supposedly able to master
the mysteries of the universe.

What if the way out
is the way back in?
That is ... re-winding the clock of self...
of so-called development,
back to its beginning
as pure Awareness.

Can this ground of Being
be our true home?
Where we have always rested
but which we have ignored?
Until now, when, with an ironical laugh,
we relax into the infantile
wonder and simplicity
of just This!

The journey continues
through another day ...
floating upon awareness,
sensations and images come and go;
providing entertainment.

It's all perfectly formed,
and perfectly amazing.
Questions about purpose and reason
bubble up in the mind,
seeking answers
impossible to find.

The answers are found in
the silence of simple presence.
The living Being which is
the Source of all that

appears in our show of life.

All our 'shows' may be different,
but there is a recognition that
we share more than we know!

It seems strange to be searching
for something that was never lost.

To find the jewel of great price ...
nothing needs to be done;
and who is there to do
anything anyway?

Yet everywhere people are
seeking happiness in
possessions, plans, other people,
objects and concepts;
and thought-based beliefs.

What would happen if they all
stopped searching for happiness?
Would the world fall apart?
Perhaps 'productivity' and
the 'GDP' might fall?

But if we all found supreme happiness
right here, where we are ...
where it's been all along ...
then perhaps the world would not stop turning.
The seasons would continue to change,
and the weather still pass through overhead.

With no desire for anything
that is not here - in our hands;
Would there be conflict? Wars?
Who would fight who?
... and for what?

Pain, disease, death ...
the unavoidable consequences
of having a body ...
would still be here.

But the little self, battling
against an external fate,
and defending an illusion ...
would fade away like morning mist;
and Life would hold us in its arms,
breathing Love through a smile!

Seagulls crying
in winter sunshine ...
warming sounds.

Our life is like a bubble carried by the wind.

Bubbles come in all shapes and sizes;

Some are plain; some beautifully iridescent;

Some burst sooner, others burst later.

However, all bubbles eventually burst.

We need to recognise that we are not only the bubble,

but also the wind that gently carries it along.

That wind has no point of origin and is without destination.

It blows freely wherever it likes.

How wonderful!

If life is purposeless,
what on earth are we worried about?

Can we not relax and allow
events to simply unfold ...
enjoying the spontaneity
and unpredictability of existence?

Instead we plot and plan;
organise and fantasise;
imagining we are in control.
What a farce!

The clouds ride across the sky ... unbidden.
The heart pumps blood around the body ...
without permission.
Let go!
Everything carries on as it needs to ....
Meaning nothing .... providing everything!

Waiting for words to come ...

they don't ...

time for bed?

When nothing happens,
nothing really matters.

Joy or misery,
Happiness or pain –
all the same in appearances ... illusions.

Only This - in this fleeting Now,
and before we can register
or recognise experience ... it's gone.

So time and space are also mirage;

no dimension can contain

Life's energy, as it moves,

flows, changes shape and appearance

in myriad forms;

an endless pantomime;

a tragic-comedy without meaning,

and without end.

From pleasure to pain ...

from misery to joy ...
we sing between these extremes
like a crazy pendulum;
judging, resisting, pursuing;
endlessly dissatisfied ...
always somehow incomplete.

Can we embrace all conditions?
Knowing they are transient and
essentially meaningless?
Playing the 'game' in the dream of our lives ...
we see that nothing is real;
apart from That which sees?

The Awareness that is our true nature
contains all states, experiences
and phenomena ...
and is never touched by them;
never contaminated.
We wipe the screen clean;
and carry on.

Believing thoughts is a bad habit.
Leave them alone!
70,000 a day is enough to cope with,
without constructing stories around them.

So watch them if you will...
then let them fade away.
The space between them is more vital.
Here the vast potential of living
is waiting to manifest
in appearances and perceptions.

Rest in this space if you can,
watching Awareness Itself.
It's nothing special ...
but that's Its beauty.

**Winter sunlight.
Few leaves left ...
The sky appears!**

The only thing I know
    is that I know nothing.
    Belief is lazy thinking ...
        dogma is for fools ...
the world wallows in ignorance.

Whatever thought, feeling
    or sensation arises ...
all passes, and what is left behind
    defies understanding.
    Refusing to believe in belief,
      I sit and wait,
        watching quietly.

Christmas shopping ...
    wrapping presents ...
        buying love with gifts?

Every time you do something ...
it is the first and last time
that you will do that.
No moment repeats itself.

Even this breath is
your first and last breath ...
appreciate it!

Look at the sky ...
Your partner ...
Your hand ...
They will never
look just like this
ever again.

This cup of tea ...
This Brahms symphony ...
All are newly born ...
Appearing here and now
Just for you!

The wind outside blows away
this tired old year -
fresh life arriving with each gust.

States and experiences come and go ...
Being remains ...
impersonal and unchanging.

Whoever you think you are ... you're not.
Find an image of yourself
that doesn't change...
impossible isn't it?

Images also come and go
on the screen of awareness.

Turn towards the emptiness
and the capacity that you truly are.
Rest there.

Watching the fire –
flames devouring logs ...
energy releasing itself...
a lesson in metaphysics
in the comfort of the lounge!

The individual is a contraction
in the flow of Life's energy.

A stagnant pool of being,
closed against itself
and the movement of Life.

Resisting change,
imagining permanence
and an illusory separate self.

The fictitious ego grasps onto
concepts, beliefs and stories;
fearing a loss of meaning and purpose.
Seeing this pointless battle –
this wasted effort;
it seems simple enough
to let go.

To allow resistance and contractions
to fade and disappear –
leaving what? ...
Just the freedom of expanding Love....
a fresh invitation to laugh and BE!

**God is looking for you –
Stop hiding!**

Can you hear the blackbird singing?
... taste this cup of tea?
.... see those clouds?
So who is not enlightened?

We are always, already home!
Always, already at one with the Self.

Nothing to do ... nowhere to go ...
and no-one to do anything anyway.

This perception ...
whether judged good or bad,
is pure Spirit manifesting Itself.

The melancholy mood ...
the aching foot ...
the grey, wet weather ...
all ... all is divine.

The Sacred in disguise ...
awaiting Its recognition,
acceptance and welcome!

Nothing exists but the Self ...
this unity can be realised
when the Self is seen
as the only reality.
Dualistic distinctions disappear
like morning mist
when this is seen.

In truth, we are always and already Self -
there is no need for liberation -
we are free, and simply need to discover this.

Our concerns with ourselves and the world
are the only obstacles
in the way of this discovery.
The ego and world are only appearances
of the Self as apparent objects -
there is no separation.

It helps to know nothing ...
anything understood is an obstacle;
a dead burden which is carried around
like a sack of excrement.

Concepts, words, ideas, images ....
all are ultimately worthless.
Just see if you can drop them all.
let go of the past ...
which is all words are ...
and fall silent.

Then, perhaps – the silence will deepen;
and open into vast space;
a spaciousness which is
the origin of all phenomena;
and That which holds all things,
is what You are!

The sense of separation arises
as the ego grows ...
the isolation of the self
in a world full of threat.

Unaware of our origin or fate,
we construct a story of a life
imagined as a project ...
a complete fantasy of control.

Steering a course between obstacles,
avoiding catastrophes,
negotiating challenges;
All a dream!

Waking up to the dream,
there is a seeing that
there was never any control
and never any danger.

We are Awareness,
imagining differences -
but always, already, Everything.

"I have many questions!"

OK – let's have them.

"Well – who am I?"

You are Consciousness

"So what is this world?"

*Consciousness also ... all there is
is Consciousness ... and you are That.*

"So why am I here?"

Because Consciousness is all there is.

"I don't understand"

*Good ... let silence arise ...
All the answers are found there.*

What is reading these words right now?
Is it simply your mind?
Isn't your mind simply a machine
for recognising and interpreting symbols?

Vision is enabling the seeing of the words;
but you are not doing the 'seeing';
just as you are not doing
the beating of your heart.

The meaning of these words is simply
appearing in Awareness.
not yours or mine ...
just this cognising Awareness.

This humming aliveness;
which knows it is here ...
the screen on which all
appearances come and go.

This Being which never changes;
that was never born and will never die,
this You/Me ... this Being!

Moving beyond mindfulness ...
beyond the practices;
the habitual actions;
becoming aware of Awareness,
and simply resting there ...
where we have always been.

Using mindfulness to experience
the richness of each moment;
to taste, smell, touch, see, hear ...
to literally come to our senses.
This makes living more conscious
and life more comfortable.

Realising the transience of all phenomena ...
seeing through the illusion
of the constructed ego.
All this is of value ...
as is understanding
the causes of suffering and its cure.

But is that the complete answer?
Accessing the silence of Oneness
to escape the clamour of the mind?
Gaining an intellectual understanding
of these ancient teachings?

We become spiritually advanced ...
subtly inflated egos ...
with fully developed belief systems;
and an impressive array of
practices which we employ
to seek refuge from the world.

Is it not simpler to recognise
awareness appearing as everything ...
to rest attention and recognition there?
Knowing that we're already 'home';
letting all identity dissolve in the void
that gives rise to all things.

Just see ... fall into the arms
of Who you really are ...
and Be Everything!

What more can be said
that hasn't been stated
so many times before,
in so many ways?

Well ... try this:
Stop! Be still!
There's nowhere to go ...
Nothing to achieve ...
No-one to become ...
and no time for anything.

Being here now ... resting in –
and as - awareness.
Observing the rich performance
of Life being self-conscious ...

**revelling in its absurdity;
its wonderful and
dreadful tragic-comedy.**

**This is enough ... and although
the body can be a tiresome companion,
the journey to Here is still miraculous!**

I never thought it would be like this ....
you know ... Reality .. 'Enlightenment'.
No lights, bells and bliss ...
just this.

Headache and blocked nose –
Brahms on the radio –
Taste of coffee –
Tiredness –
Thoughts of jobs needing to be done –
... and letting go.

Taking out the hearing aid,
Brahms is clearer!
Read or meditate?
Work or do nothing?
Choices appear ... made by
No-one.

So this is it?
What all the fuss was about?
Being here with what is ...
Nothing special!

God is busy today ...
Her will is being done
and we are fulfilling it.

The budding snowdrops;
the fly waking up
in weak sunshine;
the frogs beginning to stir ...
All, all ... are God's work.

"My" thoughts; this writing;
nothing is mine .... I am
not the doer of any action ...
everything is just happening;
perfectly ... as it must.

The soldiers in Ukraine
will either cease or continue
killing each other
after today's ceasefire...
But they will not be choosing.
The body-mind organisms, as
which they appear, have no free will.
Consciousness will act through them;
and has already determined the outcome ...
All has been taken care of.

So I sit back and listen to the rain.
God is moving through form,
and this body will soon move,
imagining that it has made
a choice to prepare lunch;

or to keep warm.

The illusion of autonomy and
individuality may continue,
but right now ...
in this eternal moment,
it is seen through.
The 'controller' is not on duty
No-one is choosing
but things will be done.
God's will ... will be done!

Letting go – this breath is easy
Letting be – a smile appears!

Each moment is a glittering prize ...
held in awareness.
Conscious of awareness, the body arises ...
and cognising the consciousness,
the mind appears.

Body and mind depend on awareness
and the light of consciousness;
they have no independent existence.
Consciousness is always of something –
until the gaps between thoughts
grow into nothingness ...
and peace is revealed.

Energy may move through form,

creating multiple illusions –
until the waves of activity subside...
the winds of thinking drop ...
and the silent serenity that is
always, already there is discovered,
waiting to welcome us home.

More words ...and yet more...
signifying little ...
meaning even less.

... and yet, if words come,
they need space to show themselves;
a background on which to appear.
This book is their home.

Anyone may enter this place,
perhaps in search of meaning,
reassurance ... consolation?
The words may speak to them
and be uniquely understood.

Even misinterpretation is a form of understanding ...
and whatever message is received
is what was meant.

The truth is found behind words ...
in the silence of one's Heart.

Spring appears to have arrived ...
birds soaring in the clear blue sky
swoop across gardens freeing themselves
from Winter's grip.

Bulbs and buds push towards the sun,
seeking light and warmth;
and frogs rest after the
exertions of mating,
floating amidst their spawn.

Change is somehow tangible ...
perceptions sharper ...
insights deeper.
The world turns towards the light.

The ineffable remains unspoken;
knowledge defeated by the indescribable;
and yet ...
in the sweet song of a robin ...
All is revealed!

What is there left to say?

First – there is nothing to do.
Second – there is no-one to do anything anyway.
Third – everything is as it should be.

So shall the 'show' simply be watched?
Who is there to choose?
Life can be watched or lived as if real ...
seen as a dream,
or experienced as a drama.

The show simply goes on ... until it doesn't.
Shit ... and magic ... happens.
God knows why!

... and the tea is made, biscuits are eaten,
the heart struggles on ...
the breath breathes itself;
and the dream/drama
moves towards its resolution.
Seeing through the illusion of Time and Space,
there is a relaxing into This.

So is This it?
Just the sensing
and pulsing of awareness?
Before the mind jumps in,
searching for explanations and theories?

Can it be this simple?
Before thought corrupts
and complicates ...
The simplicity of this cup of tea;
the solace of not wanting
anything to be different.
Allowing things to be as they are ...
Perfectly imperfect;
Delightful in their decay.
What could be more correct than this chaos;
this mess of a world gone mad?

Letting go ... there is only peace
to be found in this breathing stillness.

The words have been said many times ...
What's this all about?

Well, it's being **Here** ... not
somewhere else in your head.
Wherever you are is where
you need to be. Check in!

It's also being **Now** ...not
in the past, reliving memories;
or in the future, planning and fantasising;
Now is the only time to **Be**
... you are only aware in this eternal moment.
We only have moments in which to live ...
Why not turn up for them?!

And it's all about **This** ....
whatever is appearing in your awareness.
Thoughts, feelings, sensations ...
Every percept and concept ...

Complete ... perfect ... This!

How could it be anything else?

When the inner becomes the outer,
and the secret becomes the shared;
When separation becomes union,
and judgment becomes acceptance;
... then, and out of time and place,
Love will be remembered.

Love will be seen as Who We are
and always were ... though
we lost touch with the truth;
as the labyrinths of the mind
constructed narratives of
division and confusion.

We may recognise the masterpiece that is
our true identity,
more divine than human;
the one Subject
of the 'ten thousand things'.
Coming home to Oneness,
and forgetting the bad dream of individuality.

All is changing ...
There is no stable reality.
There are no 'things',
Only 'becomings'.

Energy appears in forms
that transition into nothing ...
Waves breaking into other waves ...
simple transformations.

What can be held to? ... believed in?
Nothing! Only the desire for security
bids us search such certainties ...
mirages that provide no foundations.

Let go! Accept our ignorance

and abandon our presumption
that we could ever comprehend
the magnificent mystery of Life.

This very moment contains all
the truth we need –
... sweeping Sibelius
and swimming tadpoles!

All phenomena are empty ...
there are no things
apart from perceptions.
The world is built from
mind-produced concepts.
Before the mind arises
there is only Awareness ...
the sole Subject outside time/space.

Knowing the difference between
a concept and a non-concept
is still mental activity ...
still dualist thinking.
Let this go.

Absence and non-absence
must be both embraced
and dropped ... simultaneously.
Letting go of all phenomena
opens the door to Noumenon.

This is all I can say ...
The rest is silence.

**Spring garden –
even the ladybird
is excited**

We are seven billion vases
full of water, waiting
to return to the ocean.

Each vase is uniquely different ...
with thick or thin walls
constructed of concepts.

Concepts of self ...
Memories of 'me' ...
Plans for the ego.

All vases will break
sooner or later;
as the water yearns to return home.

But all this image
is part of the dream
of separation.

We are already always home;
and our 'vases' are
a sad and mistaken mirage.

What if all this is a Game?
The creation of the great Dancer ...
who brings into being the world
so that it can be experienced
in all its horror and beauty.

I choose to join this great game of Life;
to move with each moment,
to love the movement
and flow of this masquerade;
and to laugh at the ludicrous
situations that man imagines
to be real.

The suffering, illness, ageing and death
that appear as acts in this drama,
can be admired as the
most amazing illusions;
both 'real' and unreal.

I choose not to trudge through the
business of living, bound to the
wheel of birth and death ...
but to assume my role joyfully;
transcending my imagined 'bondage'.

I shall dance out this drama,
performing my role in the
Divine '*lila*'.

Such purposeless purpose ...
Such unreal reality ...
Such delicious paradox!

I shall join the cosmic game of dice
enjoying each throw, and relishing
each of the Magician's (my!) tricks.

Though I may forget my Self, and
be caught again in the objects of becoming ...
these too are *maya,* and simply
manifestations of the Absolute.

The mask has been discovered and discarded;
the Real behind the unreal has been found!

At the risk of boring you –
let's say this once again:

There's nothing to do ...
Nowhere to go ...
No state to achieve ...
No time but now ...
and nothing to do but this
(which isn't a thing anyway).

All that's needed (not even needed)
is to **see** that you are the
Spectator/ Producer/ Actor
in this great Show of Life.

You are empty, and can therefore
contain everything ... apparently!
All appearances are temporary,
changing and illusory,
so do not get caught up

in their stories.

The Real does not change –
and you are THAT!

Open the window ...
let something in.
Not knowing what it may be,
simply watch and wait.

It may be the sound of church bells,
blackbird or traffic ...
each producing responses.

Whatever arrives is welcome,
for it is Life dancing for you;
sending gifts of awareness
to experience and savour.

So open the window ...
and enjoy the draught!

Over and over they circle
in the blue depths
of an April sky ....
the birds who know nothing ...
not that they are birds,
have wings, names, futures.

Knowing just the wind that lifts them
high above the houses ...
above the little lives
fussing over trivia.

They know this much ...
that this is all there is
to living ...
To be lifted higher
Without fear or fantasy ...
and with each wing beat,
waving with the moving world.

Painful stomach –

Soothed by peppermint tea

and Bach.

We live in moments, not days ...
moments without thought are timeless.

Can you touch these moments as they fly?
Being the music and not the hearer?
... the coffee and not the drinker?

Our life is a collection of moments –
opportunities to be present,
not lost in our minds.

Watch for the moments ...
they will not come again.
they are Life's kisses,
sent to wake us up.

There is no escape from what is.
Resistance to pain?
Depressing thoughts?
Hopeless mood?
All ... all are aspects of Reality!

Even when I feel far away from truth,
I am already there ... at Home.
When I am weary of life,
that is Life acting,
appearing as 'me'.
Letting go ... letting be ...
seems to be the answer.

The clouds find no resistance
in moving ... they float freely ..
sometimes covering the sun,
and then disappearing ...
the sky doesn't care ...
and loves them all.

If the idea of 'you' is an illusion,
what on earth can 'you' possibly do?

Laughter and relief may arise ...
a sense of real freedom ...
liberation at last from the
tyranny of self's story.

The wind outside blows the
young trees into dancing forms ...
fresh and new in each moment.

So this moment is always open and empty;
containing nothing of the past ...
caring nothing for the future.

Without the mind to construct new fictions
or dredge up old memories ...
there is a relaxing into what is.

Aaaahh! Nothing being Everything!

Mind creates the chasm ...
Love is the bridge –
what contracting thought divides,
our open heart unites.

Let these words sink deeply, slowly,
into the quiet intelligence
of your true nature.

Notice what is there before thought arises;
the awareness that is always present ...
allowing and welcoming all experiences.

Notice the noticing ...
Watch the watching.
Rest there - it is Home.
The place you never left.

You may lose yourself again in
the strange, unreal story of 'me';
but know that still, silent space
which you truly are,
is just Here!

One final verse to

complete the book...

See – it's finished!

EPILOGUE

So that's it ... more words! Some of them may have made sense to you and hit home; others will have caused you to shrug and move on.

If any of them have somehow resonated, and caused you to question who you have always thought you are, then the writing and reading will have been worthwhile.

There may be even more words to follow in the future – who knows? Any tools that can be employed to weaken the grip of an illusory ego and sense of separation are of value.

May Consciousness continue to speak
to Itself through you,
and may you wake up to discover who
You really are!

If you have questions or comments, or would simply like to explore any of these issues, feel free to email me at: stew154@gmail.com